MW00977113

# The Disappearing

## A Spiritual Survival Guide

## for the Tribulation

## Steve Funderburk

Copyright 2015 by Steve Funderburk

# Prelude

The Disappearing is not just another book on the last days. It is a spiritual survival handbook for the tribulation period; for those who have been left behind and face the challenges of the days ahead.

It is a step by step manual for people to acquire knowledge of the anti-Christ, the mark of the beast, the New World Order and the life or death decisions that all will encounter.

You will discover New York City's Final Hour, The Day the Dollar Dies, The Demonic Invasion and Here Comes Superman.

Along with the Bible, The Disappearing is the one book that will give people the tools they need to find truth in a world of deception. If you are reading this and have been left behind, this book will be a guide for the darkest time in world history. Even if you know very little about end times, this is going to help you during the tribulation.

If you are reading this manual before the rapture has taken place here is something you can do to make a difference in someone's life. Leave copies of this in strategic places where people will be able to find the help they need.

I know there are people that have a deep concern for those who may miss the rapture. I would say that The Disappearing would be a great witness for now and also the days of the tribulation. Some may read this book who will never hear any teaching on the last days so it is vital to get this to as many people as possible. I have included a page where you can write a personal note to those who may come by your house when you are gone in the rapture.

Just imagine your parents, your children, co-workers, teammates or a best friend facing this time and not knowing what to do. You can make a difference in someone's eternity. Leave a legacy of love behind for someone you care about. Send someone The Disappearing, because the return of Jesus will happen in the twinkling of an eye. (1Corinthians 15:52)

# Introduction

Do not under any circumstance put down this book that you have just picked up. Along with the Bible it will be a spiritual survival guide through the days known as the tribulation period. It will give you the information about the disappearing that has thrown the world into total chaos. It will also protect you from all the misinformation that the media communicates during this time. The Disappearing, along with the Word of God, will help you see clearly in a world that is full of deception.

What is being explained as a terrorist event, a mysterious virus or even an alien abduction, is what the Bible refers to as the catching away of the Church (1 Thessalonians 4:17-18) which is commonly called the rapture.

Now that all true believers have been taken out of the world, the anti-Christ spirit will be released in its full measure. As one man told me recently, "when all the good is gone all that is evil will appear."

The next seven years is a time like never before or ever will be seen again. (Matthew 24:21) It is a time of a New World Order, where all the nations of the world will be under the control of a great intellectual leader who is the anti-Christ, the beast who rises out of the sea. (Revelation 13:1)

No one will buy or sell without his mark (Revelation 13:15-18) and anyone who opposes him will be killed.  For all those who thought it couldn't get any worse, the devil will make this world a living hell.

This book was written out of a deep concern for those who missed the rapture. I know that what you are facing is beyond anything I could ever even imagine. I want this book to be a source of hope in a very desperate time. The Bible is very clear in Revelation 7:14 that there will be a great number of people who will be saved in the tribulation time. My prayer is that you give your life to Jesus Christ.

The person who left this book here had the same desire to see friends, family members and co-workers make it to heaven.

There is a review at the end with the scriptures that you should know.  Heaven and earth will pass away, but God's Word will last forever. It is my hope that this book will give you the help to recognize the deceptive spirits that have been released in this world.

On the following page is an appeal from the person who cared enough about you to leave this book here. Let their words be an encouragement to you to make it to heaven no matter what.

# In Their Words

# The Inspiration

When I was about 15 years old I had an experience that has stayed with me throughout my life. I went to church but didn't really feel a great connection to Jesus in a personal way. I remember riding back from a soccer game on the bus and as I looked up in the sky the Northern Lights were shining like streaks going up to heaven. I lived in Caribou Maine and on this crisp, clear New England night I thought to myself, I have missed the rapture.

As soon as I got off the bus I ran all the way home. I knew my parents were Christians so if they were home I was off the hook. But they weren't home and neither was my brother or sisters. Panic set in so I called the pastor of the Church and when there was no answer I was totally convinced that I was a goner. After making a few more calls and getting the same results I knew I had made the worst mistake of my life. I was positive that I had missed the rapture and had been left behind. I didn't know what to do and felt totally hopeless in the crisis. I went to bed with no idea what the future would be but I knew I was scared to face all that was coming in the tribulation. It was the worst nightmare of my life. This nightmare ended when I woke up the next morning to the smell of bacon coming from the kitchen. I ran down the stairs and gave Mom the biggest hug ever; I think I may have hugged everyone in the family. There was a total relief in my heart. I was so glad to know that I hadn't missed the rapture, but that feeling of torment and fear has never been forgotten.

So after all these years I have decided to put together a manual giving a step by step approach to use during the tribulation. This is a spiritual survival guide that will give you the needed information to know what is next on the prophetic calendar. I pray this book will give you the strength to keep the faith no matter how hard the journey is from here.

I realize that people have been hurt by a Church, a pastor or a ministry in their lives. My only response to you is that Jesus has never hurt you, left you or forsaken you at any time.

Don't let an offense keep you from serving the Lord because in this terrible time He will be your only hope to make it through. No excuse will be accepted for not serving the Lord. (Romans 1:20)

You may be someone who walked away from the Lord. Don't let guilt or condemnation keep you from getting back on the right path. Jesus is a friend who sticks closer than a brother. He loves you at all times. If you don't give up on Him, He will never give up on you.

There are millions in heaven right now that are waiting for your entrance into the presence of God. Family members who love you, saints who are praying for you, but best of all, Jesus is interceding for you right now. You are on His prayer list which includes all those facing the tribulation time. I pray that one day I will meet you and know that The Disappearing gave you the guidance to endure to the end.

# First Things First

So you understand that the event some are calling the disappearing is the rapture of the Church, and you have been left behind. You possibly have already come up with a plan not to take the mark, not to worship the anti-Christ and to set up a survival strategy. This may all be fine but you have missed the most important step that you can ever make. One of the main reasons I wrote this book is because all the movies about this time period had people in survival mode. Fighting for food, hiding in abandoned buildings and trying to make it from day to day seemed to be the main plot. But if you leave out the first step all the others won't amount to anything. You must get right with God.

The reason you didn't go with those who were taken is because they were true believers. In a world that made fun of Christians, they were the only ones taken to heaven.

For you to go to heaven you must be born again (John 3:3) and accept Jesus Christ as your personal Saviour. (Romans 10:9-10)

You must repent of your sins and be forgiven by God. (1 John 1:9)

Perhaps you are someone who knows exactly what to do. You were saved at one time in your life but grew cold in your walk with God. (Matthew 24:12)

You know you must pray to Jesus Christ to come into your heart, to turn away from the sinful life and live a pure life before God the Father. So right now rededicate your life to the Lord and let the Spirit of God dwell in you to guide you in the days ahead.

I also know that there are some who have picked up this book having no idea about what any of this means. Maybe you have never even prayed in your entire life. I want to make this very simple for you, Jesus loves you very much and if you will you say this prayer and mean it with all of your heart you will be saved.

Here is the prayer you should pray:
Dear Jesus, I am a sinner and I need You to forgive me of all my sins. I want You to come into my heart and make me a new person. (2 Corinthians 5:17) I want to make it to heaven and I know You are the only way for me to get there. (John 14:6) I know I have been left here because I was not living for You and from this moment on I dedicate my entire life to serving You. I know I must live by faith in You so that I will have everlasting life. I know that I must turn from wickedness to living a life that is right in the eyes of God. I surrender my life to You. Amen.

Now that you have prayed and Jesus has come into your life, you will need to find a Bible. It will give you the truth that you need to be able to stand against the tricks of the devil. You must realize that this whole world system is now under the power of Satan. Demons have been released throughout the entire world to deceive everyone from coming to Jesus Christ. The world leader who will emerge will be declared as the answer for the problems you are facing. But all his promises are lies and the peace he is bringing will turn into total destruction.

Consider The Disappearing as your compass that will guide you through the days ahead. It is a map that will chart a course all the way to heaven. It has been written so that even someone who has very little Bible knowledge can clearly see the truth from the scriptures and know exactly what to look for on the horizon. Don't be like the masses that have eyes that will not see, ears that will not hear and hearts that will not receive. The goal is not survival, the goal is salvation.

Joel 3:14 says that "multitudes, multitudes are in the valley of decision, for the day of the Lord is near, in the valley of decision."
Don't wait any longer; make a decision for Jesus today.

# A Message to Backsliders

Just because you fell away from the Lord doesn't mean that He doesn't love you anymore. The Bible is very clear that many would fall away in the last days. (2 Thessalonians 2:3) I have been asked numerous times will people have a ministry during the tribulation and the answer is yes. If you know the Word of God there will be a lot of people who need you as a spiritual teacher to help them in the days ahead.

One of the biggest lies of Satan is that God has turned His back on you because you failed Him. But God is merciful and will use you in this time of harvest. I especially want to encourage you who are ministers that find yourself in the tribulation. You can still be a minister for God. You can have a productive ministry if you give yourself totally to winning souls. Imagine the countless number of people who don't have a clue about what is going on right now. Since you have known the scriptures for many years, God can take that knowledge to set other people free.

Even if you get ridiculed by some because you missed the rapture, you will be accepted by so many more that are desperate to know what will be the most important steps in the future.

The Bible lets us know that God is a restorer. Just because you fail doesn't mean He is done with you. Peter denied the Lord but was a pillar of the early Church. David sinned but God used him as a King of Israel. Where sin abounds, grace abounds even more. (Romans 5:20)

God is not the author of guilt and condemnation the devil is. (Romans 8:1) It is the will of God that none should perish but all come to repentance. The anti-Christ spirit is a spirit of deception. You must walk in the Spirit to overcome in this time.

In the Old Testament we read the story of Jonah who was a prophet who ran from God. Not only did God restore him, Jonah led a revival that caused the entire city of Nineveh to repent and give their hearts to God. Multitudes have run from God over the centuries but God has forgiven them of all their sins.

Today is the day of the Lord, today is your day of salvation. You can be a blessing in a dark time in this world. You can still be light in the darkness. The goal is not just making it to heaven; the goal is to take as many people with you to heaven as you can.

# The Disappearing

With the explanations that you are hearing right now about the event of millions of people disappearing at the same time around the entire globe, it should be stated that there is only one explanation for what occurred. It is found in 1 Thessalonians 4:16-17. The dead in Christ were raised out of the graves into the air; the Christians who were alive were caught up with them to meet the Lord. The promise of the return of Jesus happened in a moment, in the twinkling of an eye. (1 Corinthians 15:52). All those who were taken, are at this moment in heaven enjoying the marriage supper of the bride and bridegroom which is Jesus and His Church.

The reason planes crashed, cars were piled up on roads and other tragedies occurred was because Christians were taken out of the world and no one was there to operate things. Jesus gave this example that two would be working in a field, one taken the other left, two would be grinding in the mill, one taken the other left. (Matthew 24:40-41)

Not only did millions of Christians disappear, so did all the children or those who were mentally challenged. Why were they taken? It was because they had not reached the age of accountability. God spared them from going through this tribulation time.

I know that this seems like a total nightmare that you wish you could wake up from, but it is real. And the next seven years is going to be like no time ever seen. The anti-Christ system is evil to the core and it will have as a goal, to destroy anything good from the face of the earth. I urge you to be prepared for the most catastrophic period in the history of the world.

If you are right now at the house of the person who left this book behind especially for you, look for Bibles and other Christian literature that will be helpful to you and others who are in need of valuable information.

Just like the person that left this book here, you must be pro-active in sharing Jesus with as many people as you can. It won't be very long until evangelism will be snuffed out entirely.

Giving a correct explanation of the disappearing is one of the most important things you can accomplish for the kingdom of God.

With the deception everywhere, you can be a witness for Christ during this difficult time.

Of course you realize that this evil system will not allow those who accept Christ during this time to openly share Jesus. As a matter of fact the Bible is clear in Revelation 13:15 that this new world leader demands total worship and anyone who rejects him will be killed. To understand that he isn't just some other man but is the total embodiment of Satan on earth makes you realize that his power of evil is unlimited.

# Why Now?

Of all times in history why did God choose this exact hour? God has perfect timing and the time of the Gentiles is up (Luke 21:24) and the dealings with His chosen people Israel is at hand. Jesus will be revealed as the true Messiah and all of Israel shall know the Lord. (Ezekiel 31:34)

2 Peter 3:9 lets us know that God was not slack concerning His promise of the return of Christ but was longsuffering toward mankind. He has no pleasure in sinners perishing and gave the opportunity to repent. Because man has rejected grace and mercy, God will now deal with this world in judgment.

He gave this worldly system the opportunity to turn to Him but they continued to reject Him. (Hebrews 10:26) It is very evident that God did everything in His power to give the gospel to the whole world. (Matthew 24:14) We even see until the last hour God giving men a chance to come to Him but many will still reject His love. (Revelation 9:21)

God gave plenty of warnings that time was coming to an end and that judgment was just around the corner. Jesus came like a thief in the night and this world was totally unprepared. (Matthew 24:43)

Probably one of the most quoted end time verses has come to pass in this world, "in an hour ye think not." (Matthew 24:44) There were a number of people saying that a lot more had to happen before the Lord's return. But I have always preached the imminent return of Christ. Some people even said there was no rapture but just the second coming at the end of the tribulation. Others said this all happened in 70 A.D. But no where in history have all the events in Revelation ever taken place.

God has a desire that His house will be full, so He is very patient in His choosing of this time. God is never too early and never too late. This is the perfect time to start dealing with His children Israel and bring them to the knowledge of Jesus Christ as the true Messiah.

Jesus is the way, the truth and the life and there is no way to heaven but by Him.

The very first messenger of the gospel was John the Baptist with the message, "Repent for the kingdom of God is at hand." (Matthew 3:2)

Jesus came preaching the same message. Repentance is turning away from sin and turning to God.

But the problem is this, like a friend told me long ago, people stitch so many things into their flesh and to remove those stitches is painful. People would rather live with sin than to get it out of their lives. Don't live with sin any longer. Give your heart to Jesus Christ and be saved.

Now is the best time to get right with God. You will need Jesus every step of the way from here on. There will be so much confusion and so much deception in this world. If you don't stand on the Word of God you will never be able to make it through the coming tests that are ahead.

# The Warning Signs

I am sure that you are wondering in the midst of all this chaos was there not some way people could have known that Jesus was coming back. If you would have only known the calamity that was coming to the earth you would have been ready for the rapture. The fact is that Jesus gave hundreds of signs that these were the last days. In Matthew 24 He was asked to give the signs of His return. If you read this chapter along with Luke 21 and Mark 13 you will gain a full understanding of how clear Jesus showed the way. Jesus told exactly what would be happening before His return and the end of the world. (Matthew 24:3)

The reason that people missed the signs was because Satan, the god of this world, blinded them from seeing the truth. (2 Corinthians 4:4) I wanted to include this chapter about the warning signs so that you could see that Jesus gave the signs because He didn't want anyone to miss His arrival.

Jesus warned about the danger of secret societies in the last days. (Matthew 24:26) People never fully realized the power that these elite groups held throughout the world. So many believed that they stood for good, but in the end they were all evil to the core.

One of the clearest signs was the gathering of Jewish people from around the world back to their homeland in 1948. (Isaiah 11:11-12) Jesus told the parable of the fig tree when the branch is yet tender, and puts forth leaves, the summer of the return of the Lord would be near. This prophesy shows Israel being reborn! Imagine how great Jesus is, knowing something 1915 years before it happened and giving it to us as a prophesy of His return. (Matthew 24:32)

This was an astonishing sign to the world. God would gather His people from the four corners of the earth and they would become a great nation in the end times. (Isaiah 66:8) The generation that had seen this event would not pass away until all things were fulfilled. (Matthew 24:34)

Speaking of the sign of Israel, in the last days God would cause Jerusalem to be a cup of trembling and a burdensome stone to the entire world. (Zechariah 12:2-3) This simply means that the Jews who are God's people would be a warning sign of the end. Surely of all nations Israel was in the news every day. The entire world trembled at news coming from the Middle East. Hatred of Jewish people is one of the clearest signs in this world.

Leaders from around the Middle East were continually saying their goal was to wipe out the Jewish nation. If you understand Genesis 16:11-12 you realize Ishmael is the half brother of Isaac, which represents two mighty religions. The Jewish nation claims their place in the lineage of Abraham through Isaac, while the Muslims claim their lineage through Ishmael. These both believe the land of Israel belongs to them and are willing to die in their desire to have sole ownership. There will be no peace until this conflict is resolved.

The signs in the weather were almost a constant occurrence. The news was continually giving reports of the coldest weather, strongest blizzards, most powerful hurricanes and biggest outbreaks of tornadoes.

Jesus said in Luke 21:11 we would see fearful sights in the sky. I would think that September 11, 2001 qualifies as a fulfillment to this verse. The prophet Joel foretold the sun being turned to darkness and the moon turning to blood before the great and terrible day of the Lord. (Joel 2:31) As I looked at the blood moon with my wife one night I thought to myself I wonder how many even noticed or cared to see this sign. I asked people if they had seen the blood moon and most responded they didn't even know a blood moon was suppose to appear that night.

God gave the warning signs over and over again but only those who knew the Word of God could see the signs. God declares the end from the beginning to show His greatness to the world. (Isaiah 46:10)

In Matthew 24:7 Jesus warned of pestilences on the earth. There were killer bees and locust swarms in the news.

You heard of rat infestation in Australia of Biblical proportions. People said these things have always been and will always be so they dismissed any preaching that these were all signs from God.

These are the signs we have seen in the world over the past few years: wars and rumors of wars, earthquakes, tsunamis, famines, diseases, false teachers, nations crying for peace, violence, sin abounding, a great falling away, and Christians being killed for their faith in Christ. Although some would say these things have been happening for centuries, there has never been a time in history that they have occurred as often as we have witnessed recently.

In Mark 13:29 Jesus says that when you see these signs, He is at the door.

He came back after giving years of signs that those who knew the scriptures could see.
Jesus said the last days would be a time of great stress on people. Because of all the terrible things happening, men's hearts would be failing them for fear. (Luke 21:26)

There were countless warning signs but the key to seeing signs is to know the truth. (John 8:32) This is why the Word of God, along with The Disappearing, will need to be your constant companion. Do not be deceived when the world is thrown into strong delusion. (2 Thessalonians 2:11)

There are so many signs but I will give you one more that I believe is important for the last days. A common theme among national leaders was a move to a New World Order where the world would operate as one. In Revelation 13 we see the outcome of this philosophy. There will be a world leader who will control all military, finance and property. These are the days you are facing at this present time.

A politician once said that people cannot manage themselves so there needs to be someone to manage everyone. Since man has rejected the true God it will be necessary to make a God out of a man.

# The Skeptics Were Wrong

In Daniel 12:4 we see an amazing prophesy in which Daniel says that in the last days, knowledge would increase and people would be traveling around the world to and fro. What is remarkable about this is that during the time of Daniel, people walked almost everywhere they went. With this great new mobility and new knowledge one thing would come up missing and that would be knowledge of God. People would turn to philosophy, science, medicine and new age religion to experience God. Preachers were ridiculed for their teaching of end times. Jude 17 tells how in the last days people would mock Christians, but I am sure no one is laughing now. All knowledge without God puffs man up where he thinks he can do without God. But if the truth be known we can't function without God.

 A last day sign that has truly been fulfilled many times over is found in 2 Peter 3:3-4. It says that many scoffers would denounce the teaching of end times.

Preaching of the rapture was considered by some to be a total waste of time. The reason was always the same, this has been preached a long time and Jesus hasn't returned yet. It is like the wicked servant that began to beat the other servants when he thought the Master had delayed his return. (Matthew 24:48) It is now obvious the skeptics were wrong. The Bible is the inspired Word of God (2 Timothy 3:16-17) and is infallible. Nothing catches God by surprise because He is all knowing. Don't listen to any message that conflicts with the Word. There will be false teachers in this time that will persuade people to bow down to the anti-Christ system. There is a spiritual famine taking place in the world. People aren't hearing the true Word of God. (Amos 8:11)

If you understand Revelation 13:13-15 the false prophet will be able to call fire out of the sky, do great miracles and convince people to worship the first beast who is the anti-Christ.

I was told one time that the way they train people to detect counterfeit bills was for them to handle real money. The thought is simple; if you become familiar with the real you will be able to spot the counterfeit easily.

My advice during this tribulation time is that you hide the Word of God in your heart that you might not sin against Him. (Psalm 119:11)

Writing this book for people who have missed the rapture is a difficult undertaking. I wish so badly that someone could have pointed you in the right direction long ago. Since that is now impossible, I pray for you to gain a full understanding of your present crisis. I would say this; even if it costs you your life to deny the anti-Christ it will be worth it all when you see Jesus. Revelation 14:13 says all who die in the Lord are blessed during this time. The blessing is you get to spend eternity with Jesus Christ and all those who are in heaven waiting for you.

# Satan's Ultimate Goal

One verse that has always fascinated me is found in Matthew 24:22 where Jesus tells us that unless these terrible days are shortened no flesh would be saved, but for the elect's sake the days will be shortened. It is shocking to me that people are blinded by the devil and the demonic forces loosed on this world where they do not understand that the ultimate goal is that all mankind will be destroyed.

This verse gives us a clear understanding into the very nature of the beast. He has the power of the dragon working in him, who is also called Lucifer. (Isaiah 14:12) Love is not possible in the heart of Satan, because He being the personification of evil can only hate. He loves killing, stealing and destroying everything God loves. He doesn't even truly love those who serve him and worship him. He only uses and abuses his victims until the time comes where he is tired of them and kills them.

In these end times man has lost his first love of God and has been turned over to vile lusts and reprobate minds. (Romans 1:28) The world is full of hatred and violence and it will only get worse as time moves on. Nations will rise against nations, ethnic groups against other ethnic groups. (Matthew 24:7) There will be a move toward total destruction of all mankind.

It is amazing if you think about this verse that God showed us that man would move into the realm of weapons of mass destruction 2000 years before this time period. With chemical and nuclear warfare man has the ability to destroy each other along with everything else in this world.

Satan has filled the hearts of men with hatred toward one another to the point that mankind will be in jeopardy of survival. To prove that this is the work of Satan notice how children can play with each other no matter race, religion or income levels. It is when the devil begins to place evil into lives that all types of prejudice and violence begin to take place. I pray that The Disappearing will open your eyes to the true nature of the beast.

If by chance you still haven't made a decision for Jesus do it now.

The longer you wait the harder it will get to surrender your life to Christ.

God has the final say in all of this. He will not allow Satan to destroy this world or wipe out His chosen people. This world will come to an end only when God makes the new heaven and the new earth.  (Revelation 21:1)

As I am writing this now, I am praying you make it. When God sets up the new kingdom there will be no more pain, no more darkness, no more suffering and no more good-byes. (Revelation 21:25) Every good and perfect gift is from above. (James 1:17)

# Everything in Reverse

The time that you are living in is the worst of times in the history of the world. A time where everything is reversed from what you have always known. Good is called evil, evil is called good. (Isaiah 5:20) All perversion is accepted in this new age. Sexuality will be transformed into the philosophy that anything goes. It will be a society given over to sorceries which is drug use and dabbling in the occult. (Revelation 9:21)

You will hear that those who were Christians were evil and were taken out of this world because they were haters. It will be stated that anyone who stands for traditional family values is out of touch with reality. The laws will be changed where children will not be protected from sexual predators. All forms of perversion are explained as normal behavior. The world is now under the power of the wicked one. (1 John 5:19)

Since the anti-Christ is called the man of lawlessness it will be taken to the extreme. Every rule will be revised, every law will be re-written. (Daniel 7:25)

Every standard will be torn down and every vile thing will become the new standards. The foundations will be destroyed. (Psalm 11:3) People will have their conscience seared where they will do evil with no concern in their hearts and minds. (2 Timothy 4:2)

Jesus told how that His followers would be killed and those who murdered them would say they were doing a service to God. (John 16:2) As you try to live for Jesus you will see that good cannot co-exist with evil. The evil of this world will do everything in their power to destroy things that are good. The doctrines of devils will replace the word of God in this time of total confusion. (1Timothy 4:1)

He is called the man of sin, the son of perdition in 2 Thessalonians 2:3.

The forces of evil have been released in great power and everything that once stood as good now will stand as bad. If you don't participate in the evil you will be arrested and killed. That is the goal of lawlessness, to make it where nothing can stand against any evil act that someone wants to commit.

But even though God has given this time to Satan to have dominion in the world you need to understand that God is still in control. Jesus is exalted to the right hand of the Father and will return at the second coming to rule this earth. As a Christian you have nothing to fear. (2 Timothy 1:7)

At the very end you will be part of a great company of believers.

The punishments on this world are coming because men loved darkness over light. "Even as Sodom and Gomorrah, and the cities about them in like manner, giving themselves over to fornication, and going after strange flesh, are set forth for an example, suffering the vengeance of eternal fire." (Jude 7)

# What's Next

According to 2 Thessalonians 2:6-8, the Church with the power of the Spirit of God was the restraining influence in this world. Now that the believers are gone, the world is ready for the man of sin to put in place his policies of evil. He will magnify himself in his heart as being greater than God. There will be no restraints on any evil; the entire world will be given over to wickedness like never seen before in the history of mankind.

With all the troubles in the world every nation is crying for peace and order, especially between Israel and those nations that oppose it. The anti-Christ according to Daniel 8:23-25 will be a great intellectual who has an understanding of how to get things done. He will set up a peace plan, which is a seven year covenant that will settle the problems of the Middle East. He will cause the world to prosper again, and for a time seemingly get the world working in harmony with each other.

The rulers of every nation will be so pleased with this man's abilities to resolve world conflict that they will, in one accord, make him not only leader but God of this world. He will be worshipped as the true Messiah.

The marking system is initiated where loyalty to this man will be a requirement. There will be no way of purchasing anything without this mark. This world will become a police state in which the military will be in charge of keeping order. Those who oppose this system are considered dangerous and will be arrested.

Here's where your new life in Christ is going to be tested. As I have mentioned earlier, this book is a spiritual survival guide written to give you the keys to making it to heaven. It is not a physical survival guide, those who reject the anti-Christ will be martyrs. You will join a long list of saints throughout the centuries who have given their lives for serving Jesus. The good news is that this life is temporary but heaven is eternal.

Jesus said in Mark 13:12 that family members would betray one another and some would even turn their own family members over to the authorities to be killed. This is exactly what is about to start happening. When people discover those who have a faith in Christ they will hate them even if they at one time were friends. The world you are living in is one where the love of many has gone cold.

God can give you the strength that you need for every test. Fight the good fight of faith. "Trust in the Lord with all your heart and lean not on your own understanding, in all your ways acknowledge Him, and He shall direct your paths."
(Proverbs 3:5-6)

# Gog and Magog

Most people have heard about the battle of Armageddon. This war will be at the very end of the tribulation period. But there is another war that is a great sign in these last days. In Ezekiel chapters 38 & 39, we read the description of the Gog and Magog war. Gog is the leader, and Magog is the country which is generally accepted to be Russia. The other nations to join in are Iran, Iraq, Germany, China and several more in the Middle East. They will have a desire to attack the place with no walls. (Ezekiel 38:11)

As these nations come up against Jerusalem to take the wealth of Israel away as the spoils of war, Jehovah God will arise to protect the Jewish nation and will totally destroy all but a sixth of these armies. It will be such a complete victory that the vultures will gather to eat the dead bodies that will be scattered over the land. (Ezekiel 39:4)

This hatred of Israel is nothing new for the Jewish people. An understanding of the Word of God will give you a glimpse into why this is taking place. When Jesus was crucified by the Roman government it was the religious leaders in Israel who demanded his death. When Pilate washed his hands of the crucifixion, the Jews said, "let His blood be on us and on our children." (Matthew 27:25) From that time on it has been fulfilled, as the Jews have been abused by several nations over the years. This anti-Jewish spirit will come to its greatest heights in the tribulation.

The hatred will be intensified by the anti-Christ. This world leader who is actually Satan in the flesh will have as an ultimate goal to destroy the entire Jewish population. His hatred of Jews and Christians will be witnessed in his pursuit of anyone who doesn't bow before him and declare him to be God.

I feel this is so vital to include in this guide because you fully can see how that God foretold every single event in this world thousands of years before it happened.

If someone told you something that was going to happen in a few weeks and got it right that would be incredible.

God told things that would happen 2000 years in advance and they are happening before our very eyes.

The Disappearing will give you the faith building tools you need in this final stage of history. As you gain a full understanding of all that God has revealed in His Word it will strengthen your faith for the battles ahead. I pray it will help you in the greatest test you will ever face in your life.

# Here Comes Superman

When I was a kid everyone loved superman because he was always there to save the world. He was good, humble, and loved people. The Bible says a world leader will emerge that many will call a superman. He won't appear to be evil but comes as an angel of light. (2 Corinthians 11:14) He will come from among the other world leaders but will be superior to all of them. Daniel 7:8 calls him the little horn that rises out from the rest of the leaders.

 The most critical thing you must understand is that this man is the anti-Christ. He will be called the new Messiah and is embraced even by the Jewish nation at the beginning. He will have a false prophet working with him who demands that everyone must worship this man because of the big event that will take place, which is going to be that he will be killed and come back to life. (Revelation 13:3)

Not only will he do supernatural things to deceive the world into believing he is the answer to the problems they are facing, everything he does will turn to gold. He will have the answers to all the problems and people will praise him for his leadership. (Daniel 8:25)

His biggest achievement is the seven year covenant between Israel and their enemies. But when he sits in the temple and declares himself to be God all hell will break loose. This is the abomination of desolation that is found in Daniel 9:27. It is when the Jews reject this man that he sets out to destroy them with the support of the other nations of the world.

This is where his true colors begin to show, as he demands everyone to serve and worship him or be killed. (Revelation 13:15) He will wage an all out effort to kill every Jew and of course all those who have accepted Christ and refused to take the mark of the beast. Using the media his image will be on every television, computer and phone which will direct people throughout the day to worship him. Here is where this book can save you from making the biggest mistake of your life.

He will demand total allegiance by taking his mark on your forehead or palm. To take this mark is the end of the line for anyone who wants to make it to heaven. It is the selling of your soul to Satan which has been his goal since the Garden of Eden. (Revelation 14:11) He is the false Christ that Jesus warned about because he will deny Jesus as the true Messiah. (1 John 4:3)

One final warning about this man is needed, and that is he will be the greatest speaker since the time Jesus walked this earth. The crowds will be transfixed by his every word. (Daniel 7:8, 11:36) It is nearly impossible to think that he is evil because the world will be totally convinced that he is good. The only protection you have is your knowledge of God's Word because he will speak the very opposite of what God says.

By now I am sure you realize that the anti-Christ is a counterfeit Christ. He has the same message that Jesus had; that he has come to save the world. But as always his real motive is destruction. And according to Daniel 8:24, "he will destroy wonderfully." Even the peace he brings is a lie. 1 Thessalonians 5:3 says "When they are saying, peace and safety, sudden destruction will come."

You may be wondering why I am using so many scriptures from the book of Daniel. The words of this prophetic book were to be sealed up until the end. It will all be fulfilled in this time. (Daniel 12:4)

In the second chapter of Daniel God gave him the interpretation to Nebuchadnezzar's end time dream. Daniel gave the exact order of all the nations that would rule the world up until our present age. The last kingdom was represented by the feet of a statue that was made of iron mixed with clay. The ten toes were also iron mixed with clay. This was to reveal that the last day kingdom would not be one nation ruling the world but a confederation of nations.

For people who deny the reliability of the Bible, how could God show us that a group of leaders from various nations would be in control of decisions over the entire world 2500 years in advance of our time? With powerful organizations like the United Nations, European Union, and various coalitions, it seems that God once again is always 100% right in everything He says. Since God knows everything before it is going to happen then don't you think you should put your trust in Him?

# The Desire of Women

One more fact about the anti-Christ is found in Daniel 11:37 where we read that he will not regard the desire of women. There are three popular views to what this statement means. I am under the opinion that all three will apply to this last day leader.

The first is population control in which the anti-Christ will not allow women to have children. To show just how evil this beast really is he will seek to control the world population by abortion and forced birth control. He will not regard the desire of women to give birth to children in an attempt to depopulate the world. His ultimate aim is to have a manageable number of people in the world to facilitate his world wide domination. I feel so sorry for any woman who is buying into the new age system that doesn't realize that the devil will control every aspect of life to the point of deciding how many children can be born during the tribulation.

Just like Hitler's vision years ago, he will euthanize the old, the sick, and the poor that are considered worthless to the system. Some have even projected that he will try to reduce the world population to less than five hundred million people worldwide.

The second is that the anti-Christ will be a homosexual and will have no desire for a relationship with a woman, or that he is part of a religion that doesn't allow getting married and holding a leadership office. (1Timothy 4:3) God judged Sodom and Gomorrah with fire from heaven. He loves the sinner but hates the sin. (Luke 17:29-30)

The third opinion is truly the worst for women who face this time. It is that the anti-Christ is an egocentric narcissist who has such a high opinion of himself that he will consider women as nothing. As Jesus promoted women throughout his ministry, the anti-Christ will demote women to a place of total insignificance. Women will be disregarded from holding any prominence in this world. A male chauvinistic leadership will use and abuse women during this time.

As you look at these three opinions it is quite obvious that all three could apply to the anti-Christ. He will be above all rules and will consider himself above all Gods. This is a clear picture of who you will be dealing with in the days ahead. Only through God can anyone stand spiritually as this world deteriorates with every passing day.

# The Seven Year Covenant

Daniel 9:27 is one of the most important verses in the Bible. It is a description of the very time you are living in right now. Daniel's 70<sup>th</sup> week is really a seven year period of time. The seven year peace covenant between Israel and its enemies is the time known as the tribulation.

This verse gives essential facts that you must understand. This peace covenant is the solution to the world's problems. If Israel and the rest of the world can get along there will be ultimate peace on earth. But this contract is counterfeit. The anti-Christ is just using this time to gain more power before he commits the abomination where the Jews reject him. This takes place in the middle of the tribulation at the 3½ year mark.

The anti-Christ will prove his true colors and go out to destroy the Jewish nation, which was his ultimate goal from the very beginning. As God's chosen people, Satan has always hated the Jews. So the anti-Christ, filled with the power of the dragon, (the devil) will unite the entire world in an effort to destroy the Jews. But the Jews being sealed by God will be protected and this entire period known as the tribulation will culminate in the battle of Armageddon.

When the anti-Christ stops the daily sacrifices and demands that all worship is given completely to him, God then steps onto the scene with judgments.

As you gain an understanding of the book of Revelation you realize that these judgments will destroy a large part of the world population. This isn't because God desires men to perish, but sin must be punished if it is not repented of. This world refuses to repent of their sins, so God has no other choice than to bring judgment against Satan and those who reject His offer of salvation through Jesus Christ His Son.

You may be wondering why you've never heard this before, you may have gone to Church and not been given this information. Many preachers just didn't feel the teaching of end times necessary. If the truth be known, understanding the end times is the most important thing you can know. This spiritual guide is for that very purpose.

If by chance you are reading this before the rapture has taken place, I urge you to gain this understanding and share it with as many people as you can. Your witness could make the difference in their lives. I pray this book helps you see the great importance of eschatology, which is the study of end times.

If you know that you have a son or daughter, a parent, a best friend, a co-worker who will encounter this terrible time, then do something about it by placing a copy of this book in a visible location at your home, in your car or at your workplace so that they will not be left here all alone with no idea about what to do. You can provide them with the help they desperately need during the tribulation.

As I was writing The Disappearing I realized that this book is a deception decoder. It separates what is truth from the millions of lies that will be coming through every media outlet in the world. Do your part in reaching souls, get as many copies as you can and distribute them to as many people before the rapture takes place.

I talked with people today that are some of the finest Christians you could meet that didn't have a clue about one thing in this book. God didn't leave us to face this time without knowing every detail of what would transpire. Read The Disappearing as many times as needed in order to gain a full understanding of all that you will experience in the days ahead. I am a voice crying in the wilderness and God has raised me up to be a watchman in these last days. (Ezekiel 3:17)

# Israel Center Stage

One of the most significant verses in the Bible in relationship to what is happening right now in the world is found in Luke 21:24 that states, "Until the time of the Gentiles is fulfilled." Jesus came into Jerusalem on Palm Sunday to be received as the Messiah only to be crucified by the religious leaders of His day. Because of the Jews rejecting Jesus, God began a new dispensation of the Church which was mainly Gentile believers. This is called a mystery to some because even though God had His chosen people, He always had a plan to include the Gentile nations. (Ephesians 3:4-6)

For 2000 years God built the Church through faith in Jesus Christ as the Jews held onto their lineage back to father Abraham. This rejection has continued even to the point that only a few Messianic Jews were taken in the rapture. The rest of the Jewish nation has been left behind. But the good news is that this time is their time.

God will use this time period to bring about the fulfillment of prophesy, that everyone would know the Lord. (Jeremiah 31:34) This is a time where the Jews will first be deceived by the anti-Christ but then come to a point where they recognize him to be an imposter. They will have their eyes opened to the truth that Jesus Christ is the way to God. God seals these Jews and uses two mighty prophets to be a witness in the world. This is why the tribulation is called the time of Jacob's trouble. (Jeremiah 30:7) When you see Jerusalem surrounded by enemies you will know it is the last days. (Luke 21:20)

The anti-Christ will make war with them because of their rejection of him as God. It will be the beginning of the end for those who have pledged allegiance to the New World Order. God will pour out His wrath on this world with 21 different judgments. They are called seven seals, seven trumpets and seven vials to be poured out on the world. The Jews will be protected from these judgments of God.

Some who have stated the Jews are no longer God's people and have been replaced by the Church have missed that God's covenant with the Jews is an everlasting one. (Genesis 17:7)

God truly made Israel and Jerusalem a cup of trembling and a burdensome stone to the entire world. Now the beast will use his full force to try to destroy those who oppose him in the earth.

This is so essential to understand because as you realize this is the fulfillment of Bible prophesy, you can have a full confidence that trusting in the Lord is the only plan that will work in these last days.

As I stated in the introduction of this book, there will be a great number of people who make it to heaven out of the tribulation. (Revelation 7:14)

If you have to give your life for Jesus always remember that He gave His life for you. Don't be afraid to lose what you can't keep, to gain what you can't lose. Always remember that with God all things are possible.

# The Checklist

Since much of what has happened and is going to happen is entirely new to you, a chronological order can help you understand in simple detail the events of the last days.

Right before the disappearing was the time known as perilous times. Men will be lovers of themselves, covetous, boasters, proud, false accusers, fierce, without natural affections, and lovers of pleasure more than lovers of God.
 (2 Timothy 3: 1-5)
The world was like a ship without a rudder heading toward the great tribulation. Daniel 8:23 prophesied that the anti-Christ would stand up in the midst of this chaos when transgressions are come to the full, or at an all time high. God's judgment against sin is the reason for this time period that you find yourself facing. It is a time where every form of evil will be released until God ends the reign of Satan forever in this world.

The anti-Christ will set up a seven year peace contract between Israel and their enemies. A new system of peace in the world is instituted with no one able to obtain goods without the mark of the beast. The anti-Christ then defiles the temple by going into the holy of holies and declaring himself to be God.

God seals the Jewish people before He pours out his wrath on the world. Two great prophets emerge that will torment those who have taken the mark of the beast. God will allow these two prophets to be killed and their dead bodies to remain in the streets of Jerusalem for three and one-half days. They will come back to life and be taken into heaven. (Revelation 11:9-12)

God's wrath will be poured out in much the same way it was on Egypt when God freed Israel from being slaves. This of course moves the world to the greatest battle ever known: Armageddon. Here Jesus will come with the saints in heaven and the blood will be to the horse's bridle. (Revelation 14:20) Jesus will come to rule and reign this earth from Jerusalem for 1000 years.

Satan is loosed for a short season to deceive the nations. A final battle with Satan takes place where he is destroyed once and for all time. After this the new heavens and new earth are formed with the New Jerusalem that comes down from the sky. Christians and Jews will be one in Christ and live forever in the perfection of God's glory. No more night, no more darkness and no more tears. Don't give up; a crown of life is waiting for you. (Revelation 2:10)

Knowing this chronological order will prepare you for each new event that takes place in the world. By knowing these things, your faith can be encouraged. God had His plan in place from the foundation of the earth. No matter how bleak the situation seems, God is in control.

Even though this may seem like so much information to retain, I promise you that if you meditate on it day and night, God will help you in the hour of trials.

For years, I used the excuse that studying the end times was too difficult to understand. I even said that preaching on the grace and mercy of God was the main emphasis of a gospel preacher. But here is the truth of the matter. Prophesy teaching makes people aware of how great God is. He tells us things before they happen, to show He is the Alpha and Omega, the beginning and the end. Those who read the book of Revelation are promised a blessing. (Revelation 1:3)

For a long time, I have preached on the theme of God's love and acceptance. People are drawn to Jesus when they hear the great sacrifice He made for sinners. But some just don't respond to that gentle approach of preaching. Jude 1:23 says, "And others save with fear pulling them from the fire." I truly believe end time preaching is a great means to see people come to Christ.

I hope that is the result of you reading The Disappearing. One time someone told me that I was just trying to scare people into heaven. The truth is I am trying to scare people out of hell. Everyone responds to God differently and if this doesn't wake someone up nothing will.

# The Day the Dollar Dies

Many years ago a prophetic teacher named Willard Cantelon wrote the book by this title. He projected a time when the American dollar would no longer be the world currency. I don't know if back then he could fully imagine that because of so many economies tying themselves to our stock market, that when the dollar fell it would take down the economies of the world. A lot of people have become rich through the abundance that God has given us as a Christian nation. Now that we have turned our back on God we will see a complete downfall of our society.

I felt that before we study the mark of the beast in the next chapter we should first examine the main reason why this new system would be put in place. The fall of the dollar will precede the world wide computer networking that will do away with cash transactions. The immensity of this system is beyond description. Every detail of every person on planet earth will be locked in these massive computers.

No one without a special mark, which is the mark of the beast, will be able to do any transactions ever again.

The beauty of this for the world government is there will be total control over every person in the world. There will be no more identity theft, no more purchasing of materials for bombs, no illegal drug sells and no more hacking into banking systems.

The fall of the dollar will also align America into the world system. For years the United States has been so powerful that even though we were part of the United Nations and other world organizations we were sovereign in our decisions. No one could tell us what we could or could not do. With the dollar collapse we will be like other nations where we will be subservient to those stronger nations that have a stronger financial base.

As we tried to borrow our way out of debt it only grew to a place where the dollar was devalued to the point that it became worthless. So here is the new system like it or not.

Some say they will never take a mark but without it no one will be able to purchase anything. One verse that cannot be left out of this chapter is "the love of money is the root of all evil: which while some coveted after, they have erred from the faith and pierced themselves through with many sorrows." (1 Timothy 6:10)

Satan, knowing man's desire for power and pleasure, has used money as his tool to bring the world into spiritual slavery.

A very difficult time is evident for anyone who decides to resist this New World Order. Crowds will line up to take the mark because they would rather live than die of starvation. You will have to value your spiritual destiny over your physical existence in the days ahead. Don't throw eternity away for those things that are temporary.

# Understanding the Mark of the Beast

It is of utmost importance that you understand the marking system and what is the significance in it. Just as God is sealing the Jews, Satan is marking his followers. It is a symbol of total allegiance to the devil. As I stated before, there is no way of repenting after receiving the mark, it is selling your soul forever.

The mark is not only for a sign of loyalty but is also the only means of buying or selling in this time. No more identity theft, no more cash transactions that get past the government any longer. This is a fool proof system that gives the anti-Christ complete control.

Of course with a G.P.S. tracking device included it will set up the ability for a military state. The world system will be in full control of every life on the planet. That is why the last beast is diverse from all other kingdoms. It is the first kingdom that will have one hundred percent control of this world.

Revelation 13 gives us the understanding that the number of the beast is 6-6-6, which could mean the numeric total of the name of the anti-Christ. A large number of people suspect it will be a chip that is implanted into people that will connect them to a giant computer system. Even if there is a chip, I still believe a visible mark will be seen as a sign of all followers of the beast.

This shows the true nature of the anti-Christ that he desires forced worship where Jesus allows free choice. This is the proof of how evil this demonic individual is. The devil always manipulates people by lies; Jesus always leads people by truth. The devil seeks to control; Jesus seeks to set free.

Bible teachers could see the world being prepared for this time as we moved toward a cashless society. Everything was moving to plastic and computers. Money was dangerous because it could be stolen or counterfeited. Most people never realized the anti-Christ spirit was moving this world toward the system that is in place now.

We now know that those who were called fanatics for saying the dollar would die with all other currencies to follow, were right and the world was wrong.

Here is the proof of how far the Bible is ahead of this world. Almost 2000 years before our modern computer age and satellite networks, God foretold the ability of the anti-Christ to control all transactions in the world. It surprises me how people who scoff at the Bible as being irrelevant cannot see how clearly the Bible forecasts the future. Reading the Word of God will produce faith in your life for troubled times. It is the sword of the Spirit of God; it is life to those who find it.

# The Four Horsemen

In Revelation chapter six there is a picture of the apocalypse where the four horseman ride in bringing war, death, famine and destruction in their wake. If you understand the immensity of this hour you are living in, you must be prepared spiritually because a large portion of the world population will die during this time.

These are the terrible times that you will have to endure in the days ahead. People will be reduced to just a number and for those who don't join in, the New World Order will seek out to destroy them. The two main targets of the anti-Christ are the Jews who reject him and those who refuse to take the mark.

I would suggest that you seek out fellow believers for prayer and support. I would not trust anything that comes across the media networks. It's all lies perpetrated by the New World Order. The deceptions will be so spectacular; people will believe that everything is for the ultimate good of mankind.

Don't believe anything you see or hear, stick to the Word of God as your only resource.

This book was not written so that people could survive the entirety of the tribulation. This book isn't about a physical survival but a spiritual one. The Disappearing is to inform you, better to lose your life for Christ than to gain the entire world.

Revelation 6:8 states that one-fourth of the world will be killed by war, famine, and the beasts of the earth. Animals turn on mankind in a way never seen before. Lack of food will cause unspeakable crimes for the sake of survival. Large packs of wild beasts will attack humans as mankind will be reduced to a primal existence. Death will become a part of everyday life and fear will be a constant companion in the new dark ages. Don't listen to one word that comes from this world, for only God's Word will help you in catastrophic times.

Jesus died on a cross for you. He gave His life so that you could have everlasting life in Him. Do not fear what man can do, fear only God.

Better to suffer for the Lord than to suffer the judgment of God. Being a martyr is the only course I see in the reading of Revelation.
Each person who lost their life for Christ found life. It is a spiritual life and to be absent from the body is to be present with the Lord. (2 Corinthians 5:8)

It is very important to realize the great number of saints in heaven who gave their lives for Christ. This will give you the strength you need to endure to the end so that you can obtain the crown of life.

# The Abomination

In Matthew 24:15 we read about the move that takes the world into great tribulation. It is called the abomination of desolation. Satan has always had a desire to be greater than God. In heaven, Lucifer, who was one of the arch angels, rebelled against God with one-third of the angels. He was thrown out of his place with God to earth. This demotion has caused Satan to work full time to destroy everything God loves.

Jesus said in Luke 10:18, He witnessed the removing of Lucifer from his position with God. In John 10:10 it explains that he hates people so much that his chief goal is to kill, steal and destroy. He comes as an angel of light (2 Corinthians 11:14) to deceive people into worshipping him over God. This has been his constant goal since the Garden of Eden where he as a serpent caused man to sin and lose his position in God.

Jesus Christ who is the second Adam reversed the curse and through the cross has brought us into right relationship by the blood.

So for 6000 years the devil has worked to convince man that if you worship him he will give you the kingdoms of this world. (Matthew 4:9) This bowing down to Satan has been seen in movie stars, the music industry, and within the world of politics and finance. They have given their soul for fame, power, and money that has been supplied to them through the prince of darkness.  What is even worse is that the prosperity preachers are so full of greed; they make merchandise of people in their thirst to build kingdoms to themselves. (2 Peter 2:3) The judgment of God will fall from heaven very soon.

The culmination of this effort is found in the middle of the seven year covenant. He will once again try to usurp the place of God and declare himself to be God. This is an abomination because man shall put no other gods before Jehovah. The anti-Christ goes into the temple, into the most holy place and defiles it by saying that he is God's replacement for the Jews and the world.

According to Daniel 12:11 there will be 1290 days from this event until the end of the tribulation.

In the days ahead there will be an all out effort to enforce this total worship to this beast who is now declared to be the true Messiah. It is when the Jews reject this; he will become so furious that his goal will be the total destruction of the Jewish race along with all those who refuse his mark.

As stated earlier, this is now a time like this world has never seen before or ever will see again. Evil will be unleashed on mankind in a way beyond imagination.

The Bible even says that Satan will work feverishly to accomplish this goal because he knows his time is short before Jesus comes to rule and reign this earth. (Revelation 12:12)

# Babylon the Great

The anti-Christ system is the Satanic, humanist new age theology that says we can build without God. It traces its origin back to the tower of Babel found in Genesis 11:9. In Revelation chapters 17 and 18 we see God judging the great city of Babylon. It is a city that made the nations of the world rich, a city so great that the leaders of the world gather here. It is judged by God and the entire world will be amazed at the fall of this great place.

Most people in America would be shocked to find that this great place judged by God is none other than New York City and the entire nation we call the United States. Because America says we are so great that we will never suffer and no one will ever cause us to fall, God brings down His judgment and in one hour this great place is destroyed.

The symbol of this nation is a lady who rides the beast. Not a pure lady but an evil one. Revelation 18:7 reveals this nation as one who calls herself a queen, who will never be a widow and will never know sorrow. America goes from being a pure nation with the goal of evangelizing the world, to a place where God has been removed from schools, public places and universities of higher learning. God says enough is enough and brings the nation down. The wicked shall be turned into hell and all the nations that forget God. (Psalm 9:17)

Mysterious Babylon is so great that for years this nation had been a hammer that destroyed those who fought against her. Now God fights against the hammer and the world is astonished at her downfall. (Jeremiah 50:23)

One of the most sobering thoughts I've had while writing this book is knowing that Americans who have had the availability to study the Word of God, will be included with those who are not ready for the Lord and are left behind. It seems the ones that are given the most seem to appreciate it the least.

If you are living in America I have news for you, God's judgment will fall in a way that is beyond description. The once most powerful nation in the world will be thrown down violently. God tells His people to come out of this place before it is totally destroyed. One significant thing is the great number of Jewish people who have left places from around the world to go back to Israel. It is as if they know the judgment of God is about to fall in these places and are returning to the homeland before death and destruction fall.

The Disappearing is not a religious manual in any way. It has no goal of turning you into a religious person at all. God hates all the forms and rituals of religion where people don't give their hearts to Him. So as you read this, keep drawing closer to God. Let Jesus speak to your heart and open your spirit to His voice every day. Jesus said, "His sheep will know His voice." (John 10:4)

For years I have tried to let people know that going to Church, being a member, being baptized in water and giving money to help with the ministries will not get someone to heaven. What you do from day to day counts more than what you do at a Sunday service. The true worshippers of God must worship Him in Spirit and in Truth. (John 4:24)

# New York's City Final Hour

In Revelation 18:19 we see the destruction of the great city called Babylon. As mentioned in the last chapter I believe this to be New York City. For years people have picked many cities of the world but only this city has made the nations of the world rich.

God will judge New York City and all of America because it has promoted capitalism throughout the world. It has said the almighty dollar is greater than God. A lot of people have sold their souls to become rich and are part of a system that has corrupted the nations who have bought into this philosophy. In Revelation 17:5 she is called Mystery Babylon the Great because this world power was not known in the first century. This harlot would spread her abominations into the entire world, which will cause the judgment of God to come against her. I wonder how many Americans realize that our Statue of Liberty is a tribute to the Babylonian Goddess Ishtar, which is a fertility idol.

This judgment is remarkable because this verse says it is brought down in one hour. There are theories of what this means but it seems very likely that a nuclear attack is what is being described. For years America has been protected by God because of the efforts to spread the gospel to the people in every nation. The United States put forth great effort to help others around the world with humanitarian causes in their times of need. But as America turned its back on God, God has removed His protection that has stood for centuries. Jeremiah 50:31 states that God is against this terrible place called Babylon because they are called the most proud. God will take America down because pride goes before the fall and a haughty spirit before destruction. (Proverbs 16:18)

If it is not a nuclear event it could be a financial event. It could be the total collapse of the economy. It is hard to even fathom what that might look like but it seems that God could cause this great nation to become destitute. Some project this judgment to be so severe that this once great nation would be reduced to the status of a third world nation where poverty and famine would be the rule. Even to the point that people would work all day to earn enough to buy a loaf of bread. (Revelation 6:6)

Some have suggested that an event like a mighty wave that destroys most of the east coast could throw the entire nation into upheaval. I watched the weather channel one time give a situation of a great mountain falling into the ocean causing a wave that by the time it reached the east coast would be a mile high.

I don't really know how it will all take place but I do know that whatever the event is, the results is that the once great nation is mourned by people around the world because it seemed that this day could never happen in America. A fact that will come from America's fall is that the nations of the world can no longer get rich by bringing their goods to the largest consuming place in the world.

In Revelation 18:4 we see God calling his people out of this place. I never thought much about it until a very prominent man in our society talked about the evacuation from America by the rich. He stated he knew of many of the wealthiest people in America planning to move all their assets into other places and leave for good. They said they could see the coming destruction and were getting out before it arrived.

We do know that wealthy Jewish people have returned to the Holy Land from here. This is the fulfilling of prophesy that those who were scattered around the world would come back to Israel in the last days. (Isaiah 11:11-12) I can't help but wonder if this is not a great sign that God has whispered to them that they should get out of Babylon before the hour of judgment.

I love America, my dad served in the military for 26 years and I love the red, white and blue. I hate to think that God's judgment will be directed this way. But those who bless Israel will be blessed and those that curse her will be cursed. As America turns her back on the Jews we are not exempt from the Word of God. (Zechariah 12:9) Zechariah 14:12 says that all those who come against Israel will be consumed with plagues.

It seems every time America meddled in the affairs of Israel, judgment was swift against our land. Speaking of plagues, a man who worked for the disease control center in Alabama said he believed a pandemic virus should be the greatest concern for everyone in the United States because of our mobility it could spread faster than we could track it. One fact about America is that we have not only been the wealthiest of nations but also one of the sickest places in the world. It seems like the plagues against the land have been multiplied in these terrible times.

I love our country but I love Jesus more. For you to survive in these last days you will have to love the Lord your God, with all your heart, with all your soul, and with all your mind, and with all your strength. (Mark 12:30)

# The Demonic Invasion

We have discussed the collapse of the dollar and the fall of America as we have known it in the past. In Revelation 18 God judges Babylon the Great for trying to build the nation without God as the builder. We have seen a once great America come to the place of total ruin. But with that being said, the worst is yet to come.

Besides God's wrath being poured out in the world Satan will be given unlimited power at this time. The release of his demonic forces in full measure will make America like no place ever on earth. A prominent preacher saw this in a vision years ago with ponds drying up and frogs jumping out and covering this land. He asked God the meaning of this and God said that evil spirits would cover the United States when God's protection had been removed.

Revelation 18:2 gives us the full details of this time. "Babylon the Great is fallen, is fallen, and is become the habitation of devils, and the hold of every foul spirit, and a cage of every unclean and hateful bird." These spirits will be vile and evil; they will overwhelm people.

Most people have very little understanding of the demonic. Before the end times God only gave Satan limited power in this world. But God now will allow the devil to have full control. It will not be a struggle against flesh and blood, but against principalities, powers, rulers of darkness and spiritual wickedness in high places. (Ephesians 6:12)

These spirits will cause people to do the unimaginable. People will be overcome with unnatural desires they have never experienced in their lives.

They will be given suicidal thoughts and take their own lives. The very spirit of murder will take control and no one will be safe because people will carry out all types of vicious crimes. No one will be protected, for with the absence of all the Godly who are now in heaven, there is no restraint from evil being in full control.

A friend of mine told me about a vision he had of people who were watching a horror movie and were attacked by spirits that came out of the screen. The people began to beat each other with these demons in full control of their spirit. They killed each other and those who were left began to laugh as if the evil spirits were pleased at what had been done.

America was protected from this by God throughout history. Most people believed America to be a good, moral and Christian nation. But as God was removed from everything, Satan will have his ultimate desire which is the total destruction of the nation that once stood for God. Some thought this to be impossible but God's Word does not lie. It is a time like never before or ever again.

# Lost

Years ago I went fishing in the Maine woods in a little place called East Eddington with my cousin. We were fishing for brook trout on a stream and had fished all the way till dark. As we were heading back to the main road somehow we got turned around and lost the stream. We walked around for over an hour and still didn't know which way to head. As the mosquito's started biting and night was now upon us I began to realize that we were in some serious trouble. If you have ever been in this type of situation you know that panic sets in rapidly.

Since I was a little older I kept telling him that we were fine and it was going to all work out. I didn't really know how but I didn't want him to be scared out of his wits. Then we heard the most wonderful thing ever, our parents were at the main road hollering for us and had their car lights on. We headed toward the lights which brought us back to the main road.

To this day I don't remember all the fish we caught, or how many miles we walked, but I still remember our family calling to us and seeing the lights that got us home.

This is your call to come home. It is the light in the darkness and if you don't give up, everything is going to work out fine.

Most likely as you are reading this, those you knew to be saved are already in the presence of God. Here is the good news, everyone that is in heaven was once lost and the same light that got them home will get you home too.

If by chance you are reading this before the rapture, see the light and come home. If you are reading this after the rapture has taken place, this is your opportunity to give your life to Christ and make it to heaven. If you happen to be someone who has picked up this book that I have left here for you I have one thing left to say. When you walk through the gate of the beautiful city I will be standing there waiting for you.

If you can take it, you can make it.

Right now I am saying a prayer over this book that somehow, some way the Spirit of God gets a hold of you to surrender it all to Jesus. Nothing else matters in this world but Him.

# The Eastern Gate

In the midst of what is taking place in the world right now, you may be wondering is there any hope for me. In Ezekiel 44:1-3 there is a message of hope that every believer needs to hear. The Eastern Gate of Jerusalem is shut until the arrival of Messiah. This Messiah who is Jesus Christ our Lord will come to the Mount of Olives and proceed into Jerusalem through the Eastern Gate. This will be after He defeats the anti-Christ and the false prophet and then binds Satan for 1000 years. In Revelation 1:7 we read, "Every eye shall see Him and also they shall wail because of Him." This is different than the rapture; this is when Jesus comes to lead the saints in the battle of Armageddon. The 1000 years is called the Millennial Reign of Christ.

Even though for this time Satan is in control of this world, this power has been granted to him. God has the ultimate say and in the end will defeat the devil, and those who rejected Jesus will be thrown into the lake of fire.

(Revelation 20:15)

Good will overcome evil and the saints of God will rejoice in the final victory of the Lamb of God for eternity. All believers will inherit everlasting life. (John 3:16)

Jews and Gentiles will have this inheritance. This was the mystery that was hidden from the beginning that is revealed in the last days. The Jews were God's chosen people but there was a plan to include all Gentiles who accepted Jesus as their Saviour. We are now a chosen generation, a royal priesthood, a holy nation. (1 Peter 2:9)

No matter how bleak the situation may seem you must always remember the devil is a deceiver. He tricks people into believing that there is no God and that you must serve him. Do not lose your faith! Read The Disappearing, along with your Bible, to overcome fear and doubt that will come against you.

You must walk in the Spirit. Stay in a constant state of prayer. Do not let the adversary, the devil, win over you. (1 Peter 5:8) When you get discouraged just remember all the saints in heaven who are waiting for your entrance into glory.

Jesus is the intercessor for those who face tribulation.

Romans 8:18 has always been a verse of strength when facing a time of trouble. Paul said, "I reckon that the suffering of this present time is not worthy to be compared with the glory that will be revealed in us."

# A Revelation of Jesus

If there is one book in the Bible that you will need to have an understanding of in this present time; it is the book of Revelation. The very first verse states that it is a Revelation of Jesus Christ. For several years people have told me to shy away from this book because it is a mystery. But in all truth a revelation isn't a mystery but a revealing of something. The book of Revelation reveals Jesus. It is a book that every believer should not only study but be able to share with other people.

You will be blessed by reading this book.
(Revelation 1:3)
It will give you a full understanding of the greatness of Jesus, who is the Alpha and Omega, the beginning and the end. (Revelation 1:8)

He is the one who is the head of the Church and gives correction and encouragement to each Church to overcome and endure so they will receive the blessing of eternity with God.
(Revelation 2 & 3)

In chapter 4 it shows the beauty of heaven and how that we will worship Jesus in that perfect place with saints and the angels of God.

In chapter 5 we see Jesus is the Lion of the tribe of Judah who can open up the book. He is the Lamb of God who takes away the sin of the world. And all heaven rejoices in His presence around the throne of God.

In chapter 6 we see the great day of the Lord where His enemies cry out in fear of the greatness of our God.

In chapter 7 we see how God's chosen people are sealed by God to be protected when the anti-Christ tries to destroy the Jewish nation.

In chapters 8 & 9 we see the trumpets sounding which is the releasing of wrath on those who fight against the Lord.

In chapter 10:6 we see that time will be no more.

In chapter 11 we once again see the worship of the Lord for He is worthy of all praise.

In chapter 12 we see how Satan from the beginning has set out to destroy Jesus, but God supernaturally protected Him so that He might fulfill the mission of being Saviour of the world.

In chapter 13 we see the advent of the beast and the false prophet. We see the marking system and the demand of worship of this one world leader. He is anti-Christ which means he will try to convince the world he is the true Messiah but he is false and evil to the core.

In chapter 14 the world is prepared for the final outpouring of the wrath of God. It will be much like the judgment on Egypt when God set the Jewish nation free and gave them the land of Canaan.

In chapter 15 this is the beginning of the end when God says enough is enough and the seven plagues are prepared for this world.

In chapter 16 is the pouring out of the seven vials which contain the seven plagues.

In chapter 17 the woman rides the beast and is drunk with the blood of the saints.

In chapter 18 Babylon the Great is judged by God and is brought down in an hour.

In chapter 19 we see the defeat of the beast and the false prophet who are cast into the lake of fire.

In chapter 20 it gives us the final downfall of the devil that is cast into the lake of fire. We see the great white throne judgment, and those whose names are not written down in the book of life are cast into the lake of fire.

In chapter 21 we see the beauty of the new heavens and the new earth. Chapter 21:7 gives us the greatest news of the book of Revelation, that no evil will be present in eternity. For all eternity we will be in that perfect state, washed in the blood of the Lamb.

In chapter 22:18-19 we are given the final warning for those who read this Revelation of Jesus Christ. Don't add to it and don't take away from it.

If you add to it the plagues in it will be placed on your life. If you take away from it your name will be taken out of the book of life.

Read this wonderful book and you will be blessed. In this book are 7 blessings that you can receive from the Lord:

Revelation 1:3 you will be blessed by reading this book, hearing the message of Revelation and keeping those things that are written therein.

Revelation 14:13 you will be blessed in dying for the Lord in the tribulation period. You will rest from your labors and your works will follow you.

Revelation 16:15 you will be blessed if you are watching for the Lord and keeping your garments.

Revelation 19:9 you are blessed to be called to the marriage supper of the Lamb. These are the true sayings of God.

Revelation 20:6 you are blessed to be part of the first resurrection, "For the second death has no power, and you will be priests of God and of Christ and shall reign with Him a thousand years."

Revelation 22:7 "blessed are those who keep the sayings of the prophesy of this book."

Revelation 22:14 "blessed are they that do His commandments, that they may have the right to the tree of life and may enter through the gates into the city."

This is the Revelation of Jesus Christ. He will rule and reign forever. Satan may be in control for a moment, God has granted evil to have rule for a season, but if you are faithful to the end you will receive the blessing of eternity with the Lord.

# Come

In Revelation 22:17 there is an invitation to come to the living water. There is an invitation to come to Jesus and dwell with Him forever. The final chapter of the Bible says we win and the devil loses. Heaven and earth will pass away but God's Word will never pass away.

As you have read The Disappearing, I hope it has been a great source of truth for you. I pray it has given you the motivation you need to endure to the end. I also hope that you will use this book to be a witness to those you care about.

You never know when you get your last chance to accept Jesus. There are a lot of people who say one of these days I will get things right. But a final verse that has always amazed me is also in the last chapter of the Bible. In Revelation 22:11 it says, "he that is unjust let him be unjust still, he that is filthy, let him be filthy still and he that is righteous, let him be righteous still; and he that is holy, let him be holy still."

A simple explanation of this verse is that one day time will run out for all of us. We will be who we are going to be.

Years ago I had a friend who came by to play basketball at my Gram's house in Maine. He stayed almost until dark and then left on his bike to go home. The next morning I was with my family listening to the radio when we heard the news that he lost control of his bike in some loose rocks and swerved into the road and was killed by a truck that was coming around a curve. To this day I don't know if he was saved or lost.

This book is my attempt not to allow that to happen again to people I know and love. It is my goal to reach people that I may never meet until we see each other in heaven. This isn't about trying to make money, become famous or impress people. It is my desire to give you a weapon to use to fight the devil during the worst time ever.

You may have noticed that throughout this book there have been several chances to get right with God, so before we move to the conclusion let me say it one more time, the goal isn't to make it through the tribulation, the goal is to make it to heaven by accepting Jesus Christ as your personal Saviour.

Do it today, there is no better time than now because you really never know what may lie around the next curve in life.

# My Prayer for You

Dear Jesus, You promised never to leave us or forsake us (Hebrews 13:5) and that You would stay with us even to the end of the world. (Matthew 28:20)

I pray You will give each one who is trying to live for You in this terrible time the strength they need to endure to the very end. Give them the wisdom and understanding they need from the Word of God to be faithful no matter what the price is to be paid. Let them realize that those who suffer for You will one day reign with You. Jesus You are still the fourth man in the fire (Daniel 3:25) and exalted to the right hand of the Father. As I am praying right now I know You continually pray for each and everyone no matter how hard the journey they will face. Give all of Your follower's supernatural strength in the days ahead. Let each of them realize to be absent from the body is to be present with the Lord. (2 Corinthians 5:8) I pray that they won't be tricked, trapped or deceived by evil spirits that are in this world and they will be faithful to You as You are faithful to them. Amen

# In Conclusion

As this book is released in a few weeks I realize that some could read it before the rapture has taken place. I hope that it brings a conviction on those who have drifted in their relationship with Jesus Christ. For those who are ready for the Lord I pray it will give them a great passion to win souls before the rapture takes place. I pray that copies of this book will be placed in strategic spots for someone they love who may not be ready for Christ's return. I want to say to those who are great Bible scholars that this book is written so a child can understand it. It is not a deep theological thesis to expound all the deep parts of Revelation. This isn't just a book on the last days; it is a spiritual survival manual for the time of the tribulation. This was written to help people who have little or no understanding of end time truth.

A lot of people have committed to get multiple copies to be placed at home, in a car or on a desk at work. If you have family members, friends or co-workers that are not ready for the rapture get this to them as soon as possible. They may have never responded before but please don't give up on them, you may be the only one who can make a difference in their lives.

I also realize that many who have read this, have read it because they have been left behind. The people who left this book here love you very much. It is their greatest desire to give you help in your time of need. When I go to heaven I want to see Jesus, I want to see my friends and family that went before me; and I want to see those people that The Disappearing was the tool God used to help them make it into heaven.

At the end there is a study guide with a recap of the chapters and key verses to remember. There is so much more in the Word of God to help you, so study the scriptures because they will give you hope for eternal life. (John 5:39)

My wife told me one of her favorite scriptures in the Bible is John 20:29. Jesus said to Thomas, "Because you have seen Me, you have believed: blessed are those who have not seen, and yet have believed."

Even though you have never seen the nail scars in the hands of Jesus, you have never seen Him face to face; you have never walked the streets of heaven, you are blessed because you believe. Eternity is at stake so don't give up in the time of trial.

# From the Author

With so many end time books that are available someone may wonder why I wrote The Disappearing. I have read a lot on this subject and realize that some books are very deep theologically and for a lot of people much of the material would be hard to understand. There are books that are much longer and expensive to purchase and some are written from a totally different viewpoint than this book.

I consider this to be more of a spiritual survival guide for those who need to have a simple and clear explanation of the events that have happened and the events that will occur. The book is filled with scriptural references so that the reader can know that it isn't just a personal opinion on the events taking place.

Finally, it is a book filled with opportunities for people to give their hearts to Jesus Christ as their personal Saviour.

The main focus of The Disappearing is to bring people into a personal encounter with the One who will rule and reign forever. A sincere reading of every verse in this book will give a great understanding of end time revelation.

Thank you for taking the time to read The Disappearing. If it can touch just one life for eternity it will be worth the time and the effort to get this in print. I want to thank everyone who has prayed for me and encouraged me to write this book. For all those who have ordered a copy to use as a witness to others, I pray God will give you a great harvest of souls.

# The Review

**Prelude**
1 Corinthians 15:52 in the twinkling of an eye

**Introduction**
1 Thessalonians 4:17-18 the snatching away,
rapture
Matthew 24:21 time like never before or again
Revelation 13:1 the beast, the anti-Christ
Revelation 13:15-18 no buying or selling without
the mark
Revelation 7:14 great number saved in tribulation
time

**In Their Words**
This is a personal letter from the owner of this
book to those who missed the rapture and face
the tribulation.

## The Inspiration

Because I thought I missed the rapture and was left behind this book came into existence. It is my hope to help people be part of those who make it to the end.

## First Things First

John 3:3 you must be born again

Romans 10: 9-10 one must accept Jesus Christ

1 John 1:9 all must repent of sin

2 Corinthians 5:17 one must be made new

John 14:6 Jesus is the way, truth, life

Joel 3:14 the valley of decision

## Message to Backsliders

Jesus loves you and will save you

Ministers can be restored to ministry

God forgives you, forgive yourself

2 Thessalonians 2:3 a falling away

Romans 5:20 where sin abounds, grace abounds more

Romans 8:1 no guilt or condemnation

## The Disappearing

1 Thessalonians 4:16-17 the catching away

1 Corinthians 15:52 twinkling of an eye

Matthew 24:40-41 one taken, one left

Revelation 13:15 new world leader will emerge

## Why Now?

Luke 21:24 times of the Gentiles fulfilled

Ezekiel 31:34 all Israel shall know the Lord

2 Peter 3:9 not willing any should perish

Hebrews 10:26 a state of continual rejection

Matthew 24:14 gospel preached into the entire world

Matthew 3:2 repent the kingdom of God is at hand

Revelation 9:21 they repented not

Matthew 24:43-44 for in an hour you think not

**The Warning Signs**

Matthew 24, Mark 13, Luke 21

Matthew 24:3 Jesus gives signs of His return

2 Corinthians 4:4 Satan blinded people's eyes

Matthew 24:6 the secret chambers

Isaiah 11:11-12 Israel becomes a nation again

Matthew 24: 32 parable of the fig tree

Isaiah 66:8 a nation born in one hour

Matthew 24:34 this generation shall not pass away

Zechariah 12:2-3 Israel cup of trembling, and a burdensome stone

Genesis 16: 11-12 Ishmael and Isaac

Joel 2:31 sun darkened, blood moon

Isaiah 46:10 the end from the beginning

Matthew 24:7 pestilences

Mark 13:29 signs said Jesus was at the door

Luke 21:11 fearful sights

Luke 21:26 men's hearts failing them with fear

John 8:32 knowing truth is the key

2 Thessalonians 2:11 a strong delusion

Revelation 13 New World Order revealed

**The Skeptics Were Wrong**
Daniel 12:4 knowledge replaces God
Jude 17 no one is laughing now
2 Peter 3:3-4 people scoff at end time preachers
Matthew 24:48 the wicked servant
2 Timothy 3:16-17 the Word of God is true
Amos 8:11 famine of the Word
Revelation 13:13-15 false prophet, beast #2
Revelation 14:13 a blessing in dying


**Satan's Ultimate Goal**
Matthew 24:22 unless the days are shortened
Isaiah 14:12 Lucifer's fall from heaven
Romans 1:28 man given a reprobate mind
Matthew 24:7 hatred will be everywhere
Revelation 20:15 lake of fire
Revelation 21:1 new heaven and new earth
Revelation 21:25 no more night
James 1:17 every good gift and perfect gift

**Everything in Reverse**
Isaiah 5:20 good called evil, evil called good
Revelation 9:21 sorceries
1 John 5:19 under the power of the wicked one
Daniel 7:25 every law re-written
Psalm 11:3 the foundations will be destroyed
1 Timothy 4:2 conscience seared
John 16:2 killing Christians a service to God
1 Timothy 4:1 doctrines of devils
2 Thessalonians 2:3 man of sin, son of perdition
2 Timothy 1:7 nothing to fear
Jude 7 the coming judgments of God


**What's Next**
2 Thessalonians 2:6-8 all restraints gone
Daniel 8 great intellectual leader to arrive
Mark 13:12 betrayal by family and friends
Proverbs 3:5-6 directions from God

**Gog and Magog**
Ezekiel 38 & 39
Ezekiel 38:11 desire to attack Jerusalem
Ezekiel 39:4 the vultures feast
Matthew 27:25 the blood on us


**Here Comes Superman**
2 Corinthians 11:14 the angel of light
Daniel 7:8 a little horn rises
Revelation 13:3 the deadly wound healed
Daniel 8:25 the problem solver
Daniel 9:27 an abomination before God
Revelation 13:15 a killer on the loose
Revelation 14:11 owner of souls
1 John 4:3 denying Jesus as the true Messiah
Daniel 7:8, 11:36 a speaker of lies
Daniel 8:24 he will destroy wonderfully
1Thessalonians 5:3 sudden destruction
Daniel 12:4 sealed until the end

**The Desire of Women**
Daniel 11:37 description of anti-Christ
1 Timothy 4:3 forbidding to marry
Luke 17:29-30 the judgment of Sodom and
Gomorrah


**The Seven Year Covenant**
Daniel 9:27 Daniel's 70$^{th}$ week
a contract of peace
the tribulation period
Ezekiel 3:17 the warning from a watchman


**Israel Center Stage**
Luke 21:24 time of the Gentiles complete
Ephesians 3:4-6 Gentiles included
Jeremiah 31:34 all will know the Lord
Jeremiah 30:7 the time of Jacob's trouble
Luke 21:20 Jerusalem surrounded by enemies
Revelation 7:14 great number saved
Genesis 17:7 an everlasting covenant

**The Checklist**
2 Timothy 3:1-5 perilous times
Daniel 8:23 when sin peaks
Revelation 11:9-12 two mighty prophets
Revelation 14:20 blood to the horses bridles
Revelation 2:10 the crown of life
Revelation 1:3 a blessed reading
Jude 1:23 pulled from the fire


**The Day the Dollar Dies**
a worldwide financial collapse that opens the door
to the new worldwide system
1 Timothy 6:10 the love of money


**Understanding the Mark of the Beast**
Revelation 13 there will be a cashless society with
a marking system that will be the only means of
purchasing anything in the New World Order

## The Four Horsemen

Revelation 6 a picture of the apocalypse

6:8 one-fourth of mankind killed

6:8 animals will be beasts

2 Corinthians 5:8 to be absent from the body is to be present with the Lord

## The Abomination

Matthew 24:15 abomination of desolation

Luke 10:18 Lucifer out of heaven

John 10:10 the thief and his desires

2 Corinthians 11:14 angel of light

Matthew 4:9 desires worship

2 Peter 2:3 making merchandise of people

Revelation 12:12 his time is short

## Babylon the Great

Genesis 11:9 it started with the tower

Revelation 17-18 the judgment on sin

Revelation 18:7 a nation that is a queen

Psalm 9:17 the wicked turned into hell

Jeremiah 50:23 the hammer is destroyed

John 10:4 His sheep will know His voice

John 4:24 worship Him in Spirit and in Truth

**New York City's Final Hour**
Revelation 18:19 the destruction of Babylon
Revelation 6:6 a loaf of bread
Revelation 17:5 mystery Babylon the Great
Jeremiah 50:31 Babylon punished because of pride
Proverbs 16:18 pride goes before destruction
Revelation 18:4 calling people out
Isaiah 11:11-12 scattered and returned
Zechariah 12:9 America not exempt
Zechariah 14:12 the plagues coming against America


**Demonic Invasion**
Revelation 18:2 the habitation of devils
Ephesians 6:12 principalities and powers


**Lost**
if you can take it, you can make it

## The Eastern Gate

Ezekiel 44:1-3 shut until Messiah returns to rule the earth

Revelation 1:7 Jesus is Lord

Jesus reigns 1000 years

Revelation 20:15 lake of fire

John 3:16 we will receive everlasting life

1 Peter 2:9 we are chosen, royal, holy

Romans 8:18 the coming glory

## The Revelation of Jesus

This book is not a mystery as some say, but a Revelation of the greatness of Jesus Christ.

## Come

Revelation 22:17 the invitation

Revelation 22:11 no time left to change

The Disappearing a final witness

**My Prayer for You**

a special prayer for all those reading The Disappearing

**In Conclusion**

concluding thoughts to the reader

**From the Author**

This is a final appeal to the reader to use this book as a witnessing tool. The Word of God is a sure word of prophesy, a light that shines in dark places. (2 Peter 1:19)

48929233R00070

Made in the USA
Lexington, KY
17 January 2016